Beginning to END
Cocoa
Bean
To
Chocolate

A Buddy Book

by

Julie Murray

ABDO
Publishing Company

VISIT US AT
www.abdopublishing.com

Published by ABDO Publishing Company, 4940 Viking Drive, Edina, Minnesota 55435.

Copyright © 2007 by Abdo Consulting Group, Inc. International copyrights reserved in all countries. No part of this book may be reproduced in any form without written permission from the publisher. Buddy Books™ is a trademark and logo of ABDO Publishing Company.

Printed in the United States.

Coordinating Series Editor: Sarah Tieck
Contributing Editor: Michael P. Goecke
Graphic Design: Maria Hosley
Cover Photograph: Getty Images, Media Bakery
Interior Photographs/Illustrations: Clipart.com, Gbekide Bamus/Panapress/Getty Images (page 11), Getty Images, Media Bakery, Photos.com, ROSLAN RAHMAN/AFP/Getty Images (page 21), Tyler Hicks/Getty Images (page 6)

Library of Congress Cataloging-in-Publication Data

Murray, Julie, 1969–
    Cocoa bean to chocolate / Julie Murray.
        p. cm. — (Beginning to end)
    Includes index.
    ISBN-13: 978-1-59679-835-9
    ISBN-10: 1-59679-835-1
    1. Cocoa processing—Juvenile literature. 2. Chocolate processing—Juvenile literature.
3. Cacao—Juvenile literature. 4. Chocolate—Juvenile literature. I. Title.

TP640.M87 2006
664'.5—dc22

                                                                            2006019897

Table Of Contents

Where Does Chocolate Come From? 4

A Starting Point 6

Fun Facts 8

The Beginnings Of Chocolate 10

The Makings Of Chocolate 14

From Cocoa Bean To Chocolate 18

Can You Guess? 22

Important Words 23

Web Sites 23

Index 24

Where Does Chocolate Come From?

Chocolate comes in many different flavors and forms. Many people like to eat solid bars of chocolate. Some pour liquid chocolate on ice cream. Other people drink it steaming hot and topped with marshmallows.

Chocolate is made from the beans of a cacao tree. New types of chocolate are created all the time.

Chocolate can be formed into different shapes. Chocolate makers can combine a variety of flavors and fillings, too.

A Starting Point

Chocolate is a **natural** product that comes from cacao trees. Cacao trees grow in **tropical** climates. These trees produce fruit pods that hold cocoa beans.

Fruit pods can be a variety of colors. Inside, cacao beans are cream colored.

Fruit pods hang from the cacao tree's branches.

The cacao tree's fruit pods can be as large as a pineapple. Each pod holds between 20 and 40 cocoa beans.

It takes about 400 beans to make one pound (.5 Kg) of chocolate liquor! Chocolate liquor is the main **ingredient** in all chocolate products.

FUN Facts
Did you know...

... In 1894, a man named Milton Hershey started selling chocolate from his factory in Hershey, Pennsylvania. Today, the Hershey Company is the largest chocolate maker in North America.

Who would've thought this could be made into chocolate?

... The cacao tree's scientific name is Theobroma cacao. Theobroma means "food of the gods."

… Hundreds of years ago, Spanish **monks** held a secret recipe for processing chocolate. The monks only made chocolate for kings, queens, and other nobles.

Hundreds of years ago chocolate was only a drink.

… In the late 1800s, Swiss chocolate maker Daniel Peter invented milk chocolate. Peter's **formula** for milk chocolate is still used today.

Milk chocolate chunks make cookies taste really GOOD.

The Beginnings Of Chocolate

Farmers must gather cocoa beans in order to make them into chocolate. The beans are then aged until they become brown. Next, they are dried in the sun.

Once dry, the beans are shipped to chocolate factories. There, workers sort and mix the beans. The beans have different flavors depending on where they are from.

A worker prepares cocoa beans to be dried.

Next, the beans are roasted. This helps make them more flavorful.

After roasting, the bean's hard outer shell is removed. Then, workers gather very small pieces that were inside the cocoa bean. These are called nibs.

Nibs

The nibs are ground into a substance called chocolate liquor. This is a liquid substance. Even though it is called chocolate liquor, it is not alcoholic.

Chocolate liquor is the base for most chocolate products. Workers add various **ingredients** to the liquor to make different types of chocolate. Some of these include cocoa powder, unsweetened chocolate for baking, and milk chocolate.

Cocoa powder

The Makings Of
Chocolate

Cocoa butter comes from the nibs. Nibs are made up of more than half cocoa butter. Cocoa butter is a **natural** fat that helps make chocolate smooth. The nibs release cocoa butter when they are ground.

Cocoa butter is often used in skin care products.
The raw form is an ingredient in lotions and lip balms.

Different amounts of chocolate liquor and other **ingredients** make different kinds of chocolate. For example, adding sugar helps chocolate taste sweet. Sometimes, vanilla is added to chocolate liquor to create flavored chocolate. And, milk is added to make milk chocolate. Different **manufacturers** produce different types of chocolate. Some say making chocolate is an art.

When chocolate is heated, it melts into a liquid form.

17

From Cocoa Bean To Chocolate

Chocolate makers create the recipes for the tasty chocolate treats we all enjoy. And, machines at factories mix the **ingredients** into chocolate. Many different machines are used during the chocolate-making process.

During **manufacturing**, chocolate is both conched and tempered. Conching develops the chocolate's flavor.

A special machine does the conching, which can take several days. Conching helps mix the ingredients. It also helps smooth the mixture and bring out the chocolate's flavor.

Machines help make chocolate treats.

The tempering process involves heating and mixing the various **ingredients**. Then, the liquid is carefully cooled. Tempering makes the chocolate smooth and flavorful.

Once hardened, chocolate is packaged and sent to stores. People buy chocolate for baking, for mixing, or just for eating.

The next time you eat chocolate, think about its journey from a cocoa bean to chocolate.

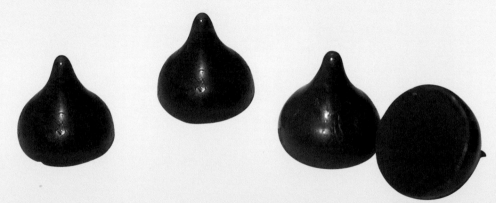

Factory workers prepare liquid chocolate to be made into tasty treats.

Can You Guess?

Q: Which Pennsylvania town is home to a famous brand of chocolate?

A: Hershey, Pennsylvania.

Q: In what parts of the world do cocoa beans grow?

A: The tropical parts, such as Brazil and Indonesia.

Important Words

factory a business that uses machines to help with work.

formula an explanation of how something works.

ingredient a part of a mixture.

manufacture to make.

monk a man who is devoted to living a religious life in a monastery.

natural from nature.

tropical parts of the world where temperatures are warm and the air is moist all the time.

Web Sites

To learn more, visit ABDO Publishing Company on the World Wide Web. Web site links about this topic are featured on our Book Links page. These links are routinely monitored and updated to provide the most current information available.

www.abdopublishing.com

23

Index

baking **20**

Brazil **22**

cacao tree **4, 6, 7, 8**

chocolate liquor **7, 12, 13, 16**

cocoa beans . . .**4, 6, 7, 10, 11, 12, 14, 17, 20, 22**

cocoa butter **14, 15**

cocoa powder **13**

farmers **10**

fruit pods **6, 7**

Hershey, Milton **8**

Hershey, Pennsylvania . . .**8, 22**

Indonesia **22**

ingredients **7, 14, 16, 18, 20**

manufacturing process **10, 12, 13, 16, 18, 19, 20, 21**

milk **9, 16**

mixing **10, 13, 16, 18, 20**

nibs **12, 14**

North America **8**

Peter, Daniel **9**

recipe **9, 18**

Spain **9**

Switzerland **9**

Theobroma cacao . . .**8**

tropical **6, 22**